Why do hippos like mud?

Written by Julie Penn

Illustrated by Ricard Zaplana Ruiz

Collins

What's in this book?

Listen and say 🎧①

hippos

grass

mud

water

Grace and Hugo are walking in the park.

Hugo jumps in the mud.

I'm a hippo!

5

Hippos live in Africa. It's hot there.

Hippos don't like being hot. They don't like the sun. The mud is cold.

Hippos like mud and they love water!

They are in the water all day.

Hippos' eyes and noses are on top of their heads.

head

eye

nose

The hippo's body is in the water, but it can see and breathe.

Baby hippos love the water, too.

This baby is playing with its mother.

But look! Hippos don't swim!

Hippos walk under the water.
They come up to breathe.

Hippos sleep in the day. At night,
they find food.

Hippos don't eat meat or fish.
They eat grass.

Look! This hippo is eating.

Hippos' teeth are very big. Some of the teeth are 50 cm long!

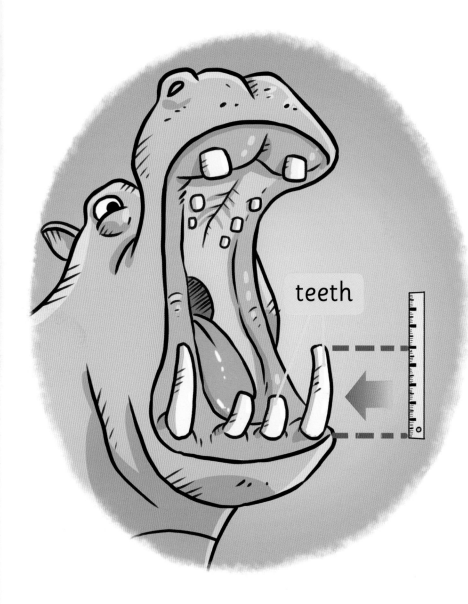

teeth

Hippos have got big bodies and short legs.

Hippos can run very well.

After a run, hippos sit in the cold mud again!

Picture dictionary

Listen and repeat

body

breathe

eye

grass

hippo

mud

nose

run

teeth

1 Look and say "Yes" or "No"

Mud is hot.

Hippos swim.

Hippos eat grass.

2 Listen and say

Collins

Published by Collins
An imprint of HarperCollins*Publishers*
Westerhill Road
Bishopbriggs
Glasgow
G64 2QT

HarperCollins*Publishers*
1st Floor, Watermarque Building
Ringsend Road
Dublin 4
Ireland

William Collins' dream of knowledge for all began with the publication of his first book in 1819.

A self-educated mill worker, he not only enriched millions of lives, but also founded a flourishing publishing house. Today, staying true to this spirit, Collins books are packed with inspiration, innovation and practical expertise. They place you at the centre of a world of possibility and give you exactly what you need to explore it.

© HarperCollins*Publishers* Limited 2020

10 9 8 7 6 5 4 3 2

ISBN 978-0-00-839783-8

Collins® and COBUILD® are registered trademarks of HarperCollins*Publishers* Limited

www.collins.co.uk/elt

British Library Cataloguing in Publication Data

A catalogue record for this publication is available from the British Library.

Author: Julie Penn
Illustrator: Ricard Zaplana Ruiz (Beehive)
Series editor: Rebecca Adlard
Commissioning editor: Zoë Clarke
Publishing manager: Lisa Todd
Product managers: Jennifer Hall and Caroline Green
In-house editor: Alma Puts Keren
Project manager: Emily Hooton
Editor: Tessie Papadopoulou-Dalton
Proofreaders: Natalie Murray and Michael Lamb
Cover designer: Kevin Robbins
Typesetter: 2Hoots Publishing Services Ltd
Audio produced by id audio, London
Reading guide author: Emma Wilkinson
Production controller: Rachel Weaver
Printed and bound by: GPS Group, Slovenia

MIX
Paper from
responsible sources
FSC™ C007454

Download the audio for this book and a reading guide for parents and teachers at www.collins.co.uk/839783